A GUIDE TO BEARDED DRAGONS AS PETS

JORDAN BONNER

First published 2024 by Jordan Bonner

Produced by Independent Ink
independentink.com.au

Copyright © Jordan Bonner 2024

The moral right of the author to be identified as the author of this work has been asserted.

All rights reserved. Except as permitted under the *Australian Copyright Act 1968*, no part of this publication may be reproduced, stored in a retrieval system, or transmitted in any form or by any means, electronic, mechanical, photocopying, recording or otherwise, without prior written permission from the publisher. All enquiries should be made to the author.

Internal design by Independent Ink
Typeset by Post Pre-press Group, Brisbane
Cover image: Jordan Bonner

ISBN 978-1-7636186-0-2 (paperback)
ISBN 978-1-7636186-1-9 (epub)
ISBN 978-1-7636186-2-6 (kindle)

Disclaimer: Every effort has been made to ensure this book is as accurate and complete as possible. However, there may be mistakes both typographical and in content. Therefore, this book should be used as a general guide and is not the ultimate source of information contained herein. The author and publisher shall not be liable or responsible to any person or entity with respect to any loss or damage caused or alleged to have been caused directly or indirectly by the information contained in this book.

INTRODUCTION

This booklet is intended to serve as an introduction to the requirements of owning a Bearded Dragon as a pet and to provide some helpful advice to new owners or those considering getting a dragon. It is recommended that you conduct research of your own in addition to the information provided in this booklet.

WHAT IS A BEARDED DRAGON?

Bearded Dragons are a small to mid sized reptile native to arid regions of Australia. There are generally three variations of Bearded Dragon that range in size with the largest being the Central Bearded Dragon (*Pogona Vitticeps*). The Eastern Bearded Dragon (*Pogona Barbata*) is slightly smaller than the Central and the smallest subspecies is the Rankin's Dragon (*Pogona Henrylawsoni*). Bearded Dragons come from the Agamidae family of reptiles which includes species such as Agamas, Frill Necks, Dragon lizards and the Fan Throated Lizard.

Lizards from this family have well developed legs, particularly the rear set, long toes which aid them in climbing and tails that do not regenerate.

All bearded dragons are a solitary species and as such you should **NEVER** keep more than one dragon in the same enclosure, doing so will result in fighting and competition for resources where one or both dragons can be injured or even killed.

WHEN CONSIDERING ONE AS A PET

When looking to keep a Bearded Dragon as a pet regardless of which subspecies you choose it's **IMPORTANT** that you make sure to do your research and ensure that you will be able to provide appropriate housing, day to day care, interaction, diet and veterinary needs.

You should **NEVER** take a Bearded Dragon from the wild to keep as a pet. Doing so is illegal and will put the wild animal under undue stress in addition to wild caught dragons being unsuitable as pets due to having a more wary temperament.

All pet dragons should be sourced from a reputable and licensed breeder and while some pet stores will sell Bearded Dragons its generally considered risky as there's no guarantee the store will be consistently providing appropriate care and as such there is a greater risk of selecting a dragon that's going to have health issues.

ANATOMY OF A BEARDED DRAGON

For the purpose of showing the anatomical structures of a bearded dragon the following photographs depict an adult male Central Bearded Dragon. Anatomically all subspecies of dragons share much the same structures so this anatomical guide should be accurate to either of the three subspecies commonly kept as pets.

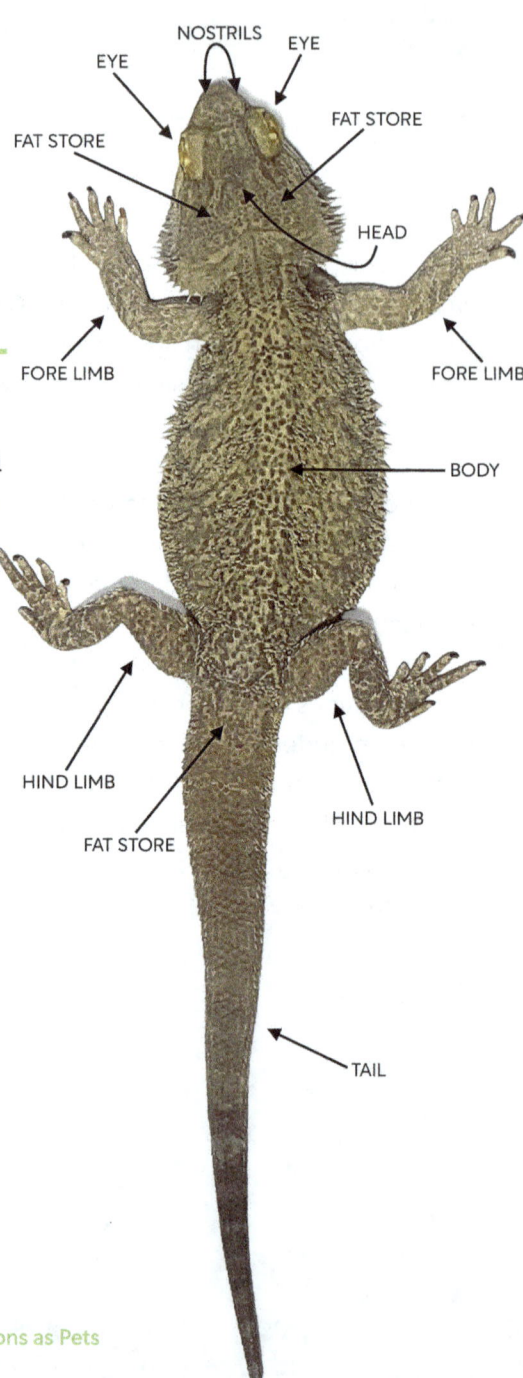

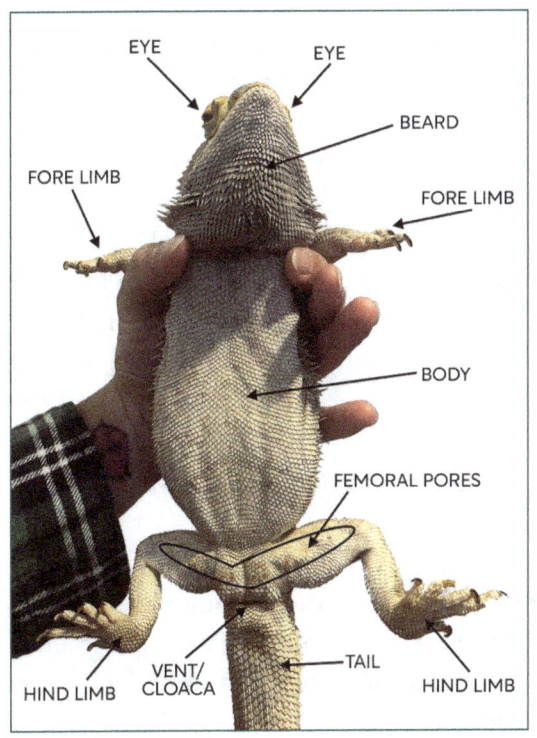

Nostrils: Small openings through which the dragon can breathe. There is a small scale just inside each nostril that can open and shut like a trapdoor to aid in keeping out debris.

Eyes: Allows the dragon to see.

Fat stores: Located in the head and base of tail these are areas in which the dragon will store fat reserves and as such are a good indication of healthy weight. Sunken looking stores indicate an unhealthy likely malnourished dragon.

Head: One of the main sections of a bearded dragon. Contains sensory organs and the brain.

Beard: A pouch structure in the throat area of the dragon that can be extended for display purposes and communication. Occasionally some dragons will use this pouch as a temporary storage area for bits of food.

Fore limbs: The front limbs of the bearded dragon. Used for walking and digging.

Body: The largest section of the animal that contains important internal organs and provides a large surface area for basking and absorbing UVB.

Hind limbs: The rear limbs of the animal. Like the front limbs these are used for walking, running, climbing and digging.

Femoral pores: Small round openings located on the underside of a Male bearded dragon's thighs and just above the vent/cloaca. These pores secrete a waxy substance that contains the unique individual scent of the dragon and is used for scent marking purposes as this wax is scraped off onto objects as the dragon moves over them.

Usually only male dragons will have these pores however on occasion some female dragons will possess them although in females they will generally be smaller in size or fewer in number.

Vent/cloaca: A small horizontal slit on the underside of a bearded dragon located just before the base of the tail. This is the opening through which the dragon can expel waste, lay eggs in the case of female dragons and where the reproductive organs of male dragons will protrude from for mating.

Tail: The final structure of a bearded dragon's body and continuation of the spine. Contains a fat store and may act as a balancing counterweight as well as being able to be swing around at a threat as a defensive action.

Third Eye/Parietal Eye: Interestingly Bearded Dragons possess a unique structure known as a Parietal Eye or a Third Eye. This structure is located on top of their head and centered just behind their eyes. As the name suggests the structure is an eye of sorts, just like regular eyes it 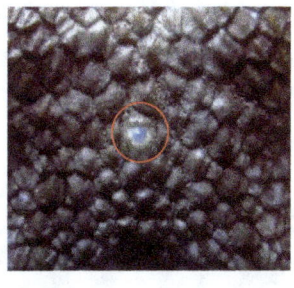 possesses a retina however unlike regular eyes this Third Eye does not see in the same way but instead is used for detecting changes in levels of light and shadow.

Bearded Dragons use Third Eye as a method of threat detection as it is able to pick up on the changes in light such as a shadow being cast by an overhead threat such as birds of prey. It is also theorized that this Third Eye assists Bearded Dragons in regulating their sleep-wake cycle and may play a role in determining duration of brumation

WHAT SUBSPECIES ARE THERE?

CENTRAL BEARDED DRAGONS
(*Pogona Vitticeps*)

As mentioned above the Central is the largest naturally occurring species of Bearded Dragon (the only larger species is a specially bred variant known as the German Giant). Central Dragons are characterized by their large, wide, wedge shaped heads and spine pattern, the base of a Central Dragons head is generally a rounded shape. Central's can reach up to 60cm in length when fully grown.

EASTERN BEARDED DRAGON
(*Pogona Barbata*)

Eastern Bearded Dragons can reach the size of a Central however are usually more around 50cm-55cm in length. Eastern's also have a wedge shaped head however the head won't be quite as wide as a Central's and is less rounded at the base. Eastern's generally have more bright yellow coloration around the eyes and inside the mouth than Central's.

RANKIN'S DRAGON
(*Pogona Henrylawsonii*)

This is the smallest species and as such is also often known as the Pygmy Dragon. Usually this species reaches no more than 30cm at the most and has a short rounded head.

SCALE VARIATIONS

In addition to these subspecies there are also 'subvariants' with regards to scale type of bearded dragons bred for pet purposes. Unfortunately not all of these are considered to be ethical so it is important to know about these variants and choose your dragon accordingly.

STANDARD
The normal scale type. This is what you'd find in wild dragons. The scales are full sized and rough to the touch.

LEATHERBACK
These dragons are bred to have smaller sized scales than standards and this results in them being softer to the touch.

SILKBACK
This is a variant considered to be highly unethical. These dragons are bred to have NO scales and as a result have a terrible quality of life. They tend to have paper thin skin and

can seriously injure themselves simply by brushing up against decor the wrong way so they need to be kept in a bare tank. You should avoid purchasing one of these and if you see a seller selling them report them to the relevant authorities (i.e. RSPCA)

Nowadays this variant is rarely bred due to the increasing awareness of the unethical nature of the breed however some breeders or sellers will still sell silkbacks which is a practice widely frowned upon by the bearded dragon community.

MORPHS

In addition to subspecies and scale variants there is also 'morphs' to consider. Morphs refer to the colour and pattern of the dragon and is a term widely used for such a purpose in the reptile trade.

Be aware that dragons can change their color to an extent for basking or display purposes, becoming lighter or darker dependent on need.

Morphs are something that is going to have an effect on the price tag of a dragon.

Standard coloured dragons which are often shades of olive, sandy or brown are generally going to be cheaper.

Fancier/brighter colours such as yellows, reds and oranges will be more pricey. Some dragons will also have markings like the stripes of a tiger and these can also increase the price of a dragon.

In turn **white coloured** dragons are going to be even more expensive but the most expensive variant by far is a morph known as a 'Zero', this is a dragon that is pure white, often with deep black coloured eyes.

DO I NEED A LICENCE?

Yes. You do need a specific reptile keepers licence in order to keep a Bearded Dragon in Australia.

You can apply for this licence online from your relevant state's environment site under the topic licences and permits.

In order to obtain this licence you must be:

- 16 or older

- the parent or guardian of children younger than 16

For a single Bearded Dragon you will need the R1 reptile licence. This will cost $50 and is valid for 5 years before needing to be renewed. If you are a pensioner (or other concession card holder) the cost will be discounted.

CHOOSING YOUR FIRST DRAGON

For someone who's looking for their first bearded dragon I recommend sourcing it from a licensed breeder rather than a general pet store and selecting a dragon no younger than **6 MONTHS** old. This is because by the age of 6 months any health issues the dragon has will be easy to spot and the dragon will also be able to better handle any beginner errors. I also recommend a male as your first dragon.

Look for bright eyes, alertness, plump limbs, plump tail base and a plump base of the head.

THINGS TO KNOW

Often a new dragon will be skittish and may even be a bit bitey. This is normal as the dragon will need time to adjust to its new surroundings and new people. Slowly offer your hand with fingers curled inward and allow your dragon to investigate of its own accord, it will most likely lick you to sample your scent and over time with patience will learn to trust you. Handle a new dragon for a couple of minutes daily and allow them to decide when they've had enough. Eventually they will get used to the interaction.

If you do get bitten they usually let go quickly. Small dragons are unlikely to break your skin to the point of bleeding but larger dragons will be able to. Wash the bite site with warm water and soap and apply an antiseptic and it should be fine. As always with an animal bite if you have any concerns about the bite or its healing you can contact a medical professional such as a GP to take a look and determine whether anything further needs to be done.

MALE OR FEMALE?

Male and Female dragons each have their own unique care. Female dragons will produce eggs regardless of whether there is a male dragon present or not, these unfertilised eggs are known as 'slugs' and should be removed and disposed off once laid. During this time the female dragon will need more calcium supplementation. Comparatively a Male dragon is an easier choice for someone new to owning a bearded dragon as caring for a female dragon during the time she's producing eggs can be a complex task.

Male dragons have a series of pores on the underside of their thighs and near their vent (cloaca) that produce a waxy substance which contains their unique individual scent. As they move about this substance transfers onto surfaces. If your dragon isn't very active and remains in one spot most of the time you will need to monitor these pores as they can become clogged which will need to be addressed by a vet in a sterile environment, attempting to unclog these pores yourself can be dangerous as there is a lot of blood supply around these pores so bleeding can occur.

Adult male dragons will also produce sperm plugs which appear as a creamy coloured 'tube' that can be squeezed out when they poop. This is normal and nothing to worry about.

In addition to this there can be some other sex and/or species related issues that may arise in captivity and require vet treatment. Below I will talk about some of these.

Prolapse
Prolapse is a term that in general refers to some structure within the body leaving its normal positioning and often requiring vet intervention to address.

In bearded dragons should this occur it is most likely to present in the cloacal region, usually as a result of excessive straining to pass waste but can also occur as a result of dehydration, egg laying, the condition egg binding, impaction (digestive system blockage) or even trauma such as during mating.

The prolapsed tissue can be the hemipenes (male reproductive organs) and could be just one or both. The tissue could also be the end portion of the digestive tract or in the case of females the uterus itself.

Some subspecies are more prone to these issues than others, particularly smaller species such as the Rankin's Dragon.

This is a condition that requires immediate treatment by a vet and you should not attempt to resolve this at home or leave it untreated. Not treating this issue can put your dragon at risk of tissue death and the death of the dragon.

Give your reptile vet a call to let them know what has happened and that you are on the way so they can be ready and while on the way have your dragon on clean paper towel and keep the protruding tissue moist, ideally with water based lubricant such as KY Jelly but if you don't have this on hand fresh clean water should be fine.

The vet will be able to clean, re-hydrate and inspect the tissue for damage then return it to its proper place and dependent on the situation may recommend further treatment to prevent future occurrences which could be placing a stitch to tighten the area up or even just recommending a dietary change.

Preovulatory Follicular Stasis
Also known as Preovulatory Egg Binding or simply just Egg Binding, this is a condition that can be common in captive female bearded dragons.

It occurs as a result of mature follicles failing to ovulate (release eggs) and can occur for a number of reasons such as incorrect husbandry (not enough calcium for example) or disease (one example being cloacal prolapse).

Some common signs of this issue are anorexia, lethargy, weight loss, distension (bloating) of the abdomen and collapse.

If you notice these signs in your female dragon a vet examination is in order. The vet will be able to determine whether your dragon is Egg Bound and if so will be able to work with you to address the issue. This can be done through physical examination and X-Ray and may require supportive care such as fluids and warmth and often surgery to remove the stuck eggs.

Not treating this issue can be fatal for the dragon.

HOUSING

Usually the most expensive part of owning a bearded dragon will be obtaining the initial setup. They will need a large glass enclosure with ventilation (mesh top) with sliding or locking doors, at least 1 digital temperature + humidity monitor, decor with rough surfaces, two lamps with specialised bulbs (1 UVB bulb and 1 Ceramic Heat Emitter), a surface to bask on (such as a ledge or reptile hammock), a hide, a water dish, a food dish, a pair of feeding tweezers and appropriate flooring.

If you find you're having trouble achieving and maintaining the required temperatures and humidity within the enclosure you may want to try a melamine or timber enclosure as those tend to retain heat better.

An enclosure of this construction may also be optimal if you have a dragon who tends to feel nervous or scared by activity around them.

When it comes to enclosure size bigger is always better but generally as large as your available space and finances will allow is OK.

Dragons will benefit from height in an enclosure as well as they are a species that often enjoys climbing and seeking out elevated positions.

RECOMMENDED BRANDS

Reptizoo makes great tanks for bearded dragons with ideal sizing and ventilation.

Exo Terra or **Zoo Med** make good dome lamp covers.

Get Your Pet Right makes the Supersun bulb I mentioned in lighting. **Exo Terra** also makes good lower wattage globes just make sure with those that you get the Desert globe if you choose Exo Terra.

URS or **Exo Terra** make ceramic heat emitter globes.

CHOOSING SUBSTRATE/FLOORING

DO NOT USE LOOSE SUBSTRATE (woodchips, sand, dirt etc.) using this provides a higher maintenance, less sanitary and potentially harmful environment. Wood Chips can accidentally be ingested and cause internal blockages, sand and dirt can also be accidentally ingested, kick up dust that can cause respiratory issues and both wood chips and sand/dirt provide an ideal breeding ground for bacteria and parasites that can negatively impact the health of your dragon. **AVOID CALCIUM SAND ENTIRELY.** Sometimes sold under the names Reptilite, Dragon Sand, Vita-Sand, Repti-Sand, Calcium Carbonate or simply as CaCO3.

If you want to provide a digging space for your dragon you can use a box or tray with clean children's play sand or even recycled paper kitten litter such as the brand Breeder's Choice. This will give your dragon the opportunity to dig in a material that is safe and relatively easy to clean and change out.

Female dragons in particular would enjoy a 'dig box' as they will often want to dig during the egg laying period.

For a young dragon or one who isn't bathroom trained I recommend something like slate tile which will absorb the heat from the lamps, provide a hard surface to help maintain their claws and be easy to clean.

For older dragons who are bathroom trained, using a good terrarium carpet is OK if you wash it regularly.

CHOOSING DECOR

Provide items with rough surfaces which they can use to rub against and aid shedding. I highly recommend a log ornament and a plastic barrel cactus. A reptile hammock is also a good investment and providing a suitably sized hide is a must. Often you can find better tank decor in the aquarium decor section.

A wallpaper on the back of the tank is a good idea and will aid in reducing stress by providing a more natural look. Basking/climbing walls are also good and can be purchased from some pet supply stores or occasionally custom made if you search somewhere like Facebook marketplace or Gumtree.

TEMPERATURE & HUMIDITY MONITORING

Have at least **ONE** digital temperature and humidity monitor with a probe you can attach inside the tank. Digital is more accurate than the analogue gauges. If you have one, attach it on the hot side of the tank near where the dragon basks. If you have two, place the second monitor's probe on the cool side of the tank lower down near the floor.

HEATING & LIGHTING

You will need a UVB emitting bulb (I recommend the Supersun bulbs for this). You may have to experiment with wattages to find the ideal strength for your enclosure size. You're aiming for the hot side of your tank to be between 30–38°C.

When it comes to lighting the best style as recommended by vets is a UVB Tube light as this will extend the length of the tank and result in a more evenly distributed area of UVB.

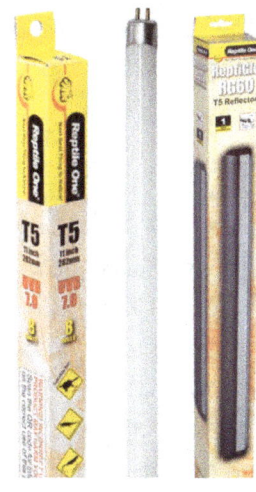

When choosing a UVB Tube light generally the ideal one to look for with a bearded dragon is a T5. A good example is the Reptile One brand T5 12% UVB Light Tube (available in 60cm, 90cm and 120cm lengths) which will fit in a Reptile One brand ReptiGlo T5 Reflector housing of matching length.

If possible Natural unfiltered sunlight is the best possible. Allowing your dragon to spend time out in the sun (in a secure enclosure and supervised) is extremely beneficial for maintaining ideal bone health and UVB exposure.

For heating you should use a ceramic heat emitter bulb. These produce heat but no light so are ideal for leaving on overnight without disturbing the dragon's sleep. **AVOID** heat

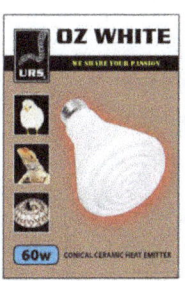

bulbs that produce red or purple light. These bulbs are ideal for maintaining ambient temperature but a Basking light is what you would want to provide the type of heat your dragon will absorb. An example of one of these is an Exo Terra brand Halogen Basking Spot bulb in a dome clamp.

WATER

Choose a water bowl that's deep enough it can hold a decent amount of water but small enough in size that the dragon can't get itself into trouble. **ALWAYS** provide constant access to fresh water.

Just because Bearded dragons are native to an arid climate does not mean they don't need ready access to water, even an arid climate is going to have some level of water present.

WHAT DO I FEED MY DRAGON?

Bearded Dragons require a differing diet depending on their stage of life. They are omnivorous meaning they eat both insects and plant matter.

Dragons from the hatchling stage to 1 year old require more insects than greens (for example 5 days of insects per week and 2 days of greens per week). Dragons of 1 year and older need more greens than insects (5 days of greens per week and 2 days of insects per week).

You should **ONLY** feed your dragon items that are smaller than the space between their eyes. This is to prevent any internal blockages or possible choking. I will provide you with a chart showing what foods are safe for them, how to prepare these foods for them and how often they can be provided.

Ideal insects are Dubia Roaches (Wood roaches), Crickets, BSFL (Black Soldier Fly Larvae). Try to avoid feeding mealworms and superworms as these are considered to be like giving your lizard McDonald's. NEVER feed them insects you've caught yourself. Live insects are preferred over freeze dried. Petbarn has a good range of Roaches and Crickets in various sizes to suit different sizes of dragon.

Every feeding of insects you should dust the insects with the calcium + D3 supplement.

I do **NOT** recommend feeding them insects while they're inside their enclosure because if they miss one and it runs off there's plenty of places in the enclosure for the insect to hide and cause trouble. It's worthwhile obtaining a large tub and putting the dragon in that when you feed them insects. Live insects can be difficult to catch at times. Crickets are easiest to grab on their large rear legs and the roaches it's easier to flick them out into the feeding tub rather than try to grab them.

It's worthwhile to purchase Aquaload and Gutload with your live insects. Aquaload is a gel block that allows your live insects to remain hydrated without risking drowning and Gutload is a granule insect food that will prevent them from starving and boost their nutrient value for your dragon. Using both Aquaload and Gutload can prolong the life of your feeder insects.

ROACHES

Pros
Nutritious
Quiet
Not too stinky

Cons
Fast moving
Sometimes not available in store
Can't be stored in the fridge

CRICKETS

Pros
Often available in store
Easier to catch
Nutritious

Cons
Noisy
Stinky
Can't be stored in the fridge

BLACK SOLIDER FLY LARVAE (BSLF)

Pros
Quiet
Easy to catch
Near perfectly nutritionally balanced
Can be stored in the fridge

Cons
Can be harder to find live
If left long enough they will pupate into adult soldier flies

MEALWORMS/SUPERWORMS

Pros

The most commonly available live feeder insect

Can be stored in the fridge

Great for quickly building up body weight after weight loss due to illness/poor appetite

Cons

Very high fat content. Basically considered lizard McDonald's

If left long enough will pupate into adult darkling beetles

SILKWORMS

Pros

High in calcium

Cons

Can be harder to find available as a feeder insect

Will ONLY eat mulberry leaves

DO I NEED TO PROVIDE SUPPLEMENTS?

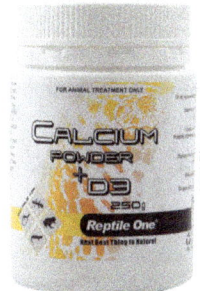

Bearded dragons require a calcium supplement. You will need a Calcium + D3 supplement. The added D3 helps them to use the calcium better and will keep them healthy. Failing to provide this can result in an often fatal debilitating issue known as MBD (Metabolic Bone Disease) that causes softening and deformation of the bones in the jaw (known as Rubber Jaw), deformation of the spine and eventually brittleness of the bones resulting in fractures and loss of mobility.

BEHAVIOUR

Bearded Dragons are a highly interactive and very intelligent reptile. They will generally enjoy socialising with people and many can't get enough of having a cuddle.

Bearded Dragons can be highly communicative so its beneficial to know their behaviours and interpret them accordingly.

Some common behaviours you may see include:

HEAD BOBBING

This is the act of 'bouncing' the head up and down and can be one or two slow bobs or a series of vigorous, rapid bobs.

The slower bobs are generally a show of acknowledgement, usually of another dragon that they don't currently see as a threat.

The rapid bobs however are often a display of dominance and are usually performed to other dragons or even humans with darker coloured hair or beards that the dragon may interpret as a 'challenge'.

That said this behaviour in male dragons can also be a courtship behaviour performed at a female dragon to signify he's wanting to mate.

Additionally some dragons will head bob at seemingly nothing at all, something that is more commonly seen in juveniles.

ARM WAVING

Arm waving is when a dragon raises one forelimb and moves it in a slow, sometimes shaky arc from the outside of the body inward, almost like a freestyle swimmers strokes.

This is often used as a greeting or as a display of submission, often directed at another dragon. This gesture may be in response to another dragon's head bobbing or as a gesture to another dragon who may respond with either a wave or head bob.

GAPING

This refers to a dragon with their mouth wide open. This behaviour has a number of meanings dependent on the context. If startled or feeling threatened they will often perform this behaviour as a deterrent to a perceived threat however they will also hold their mouth open whilst basking as a way to help regulate their body temperature and this is usually a good sign that the enclosure is at an ideal temperature.

BLACK BEARDING

This is when a dragon darkens the colour of their beard. Usually this is a sign the dragon is unhappy in some way whether it be upset, angry or perhaps not feeling well or in pain. This may or may not be combined with head bobbing and/or extending the beard.

EXTENDING THE BEARD

This is when the dragon puffs out their beard like a cone or fan under their chin. This behaviour is usually done for similar reasons as Black Bearding or in response to a perceived threat and may be paired with puffing up their body.

That said sometimes you will see your dragon extending and flattening their beard for other reasons that can be as simple as stretching in the mornings or stretching for the purpose of aiding the shedding of scales.

TAIL CURLED UPWARD

Often referred to as 'Banana Tail' this is when the dragon curls their tail upward in a crescent shape. This is a sign of the dragon being happy and/or interested, stimulated or excited by its environment and can often be seen while the dragon is exploring.

BODY FLATTENING

Also sometimes called 'Pancaking' this is when the reptile flattens its body into a disc like shape. This is often done while

basking which is the act of sitting under or on a warm surface to warm up. This act serves to increase the surface area that is exposed to the warmth and works to help the dragon warm up more efficiently. This is a behaviour that can also be observed in many other reptiles such as Blue Tongue Skinks and snakes.

WILL MY DRAGON HIBERNATE?

No but your Dragon will likely brumate.

Brumation is a state of semi-hibernation that bearded dragons undergo when the weather starts to cool off around winter. Unlike hibernation they don't sleep for the entire duration. Brumation involves the dragon remaining in one spot, usually in a hide for a prolonged length of time which can be anywhere from a week right up to over a month. They alternate between having their eyes closed and open. You will still need to provide fresh water for them as if they are thirsty they will come out for a drink.

Brumation is usually safe to leave your dragon to do. The only exception is when the dragon is very young or has a health issue that would put them at risk such as being malnourished. You can prevent brumation by maintaining a constant high enclosure temperature, likewise brumation can be induced by lowering the enclosure temperature though this is usually only done by breeders as mating occurs in this species immediately following brumation so by inducing brumation at will breeders can produce a steady supply of hatchlings for sale.

DO I NEED TO BATHE MY DRAGON?

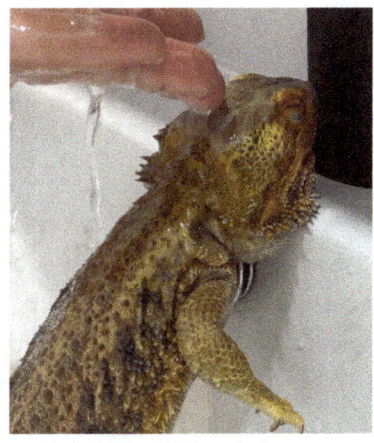

It's recommended to bathe your dragon in shallow warm water every 6-8 days. I recommend using a soft bristled toothbrush to give them a gentle scrub. This will keep them clean and assist in keeping their skin hydrated. Always ensure that the depth of the water is no deeper than their wrists in order to prevent them accidentally submerging their nostrils and be careful to avoid getting water in their nostrils as if inhaled this can cause respiratory issues.

When finished bathing dry them off with a clean towel.

SHEDDING

Unlike snakes, bearded dragons shed in pieces. There's two types of shedding they do.

Deep shed which can take weeks to months and involves the shedding of a thick layer of scales and a light shed which takes days to a week or so and involves shedding a thin layer of scales.

During shedding pay attention to the toes and tail tip as these are spots where the shed can get stuck and if not removed can result in circulation being cut off.

HEALTH

RECORD KEEPING

Keeping a good record of your bearded dragon is a great idea that will be beneficial not just to yourself but also to vets and anyone else who may need to provide care for your dragon.

One way to do this is to use a journal with lined pages and draw up a 4 columned table into which you can enter information such as the date, what food has been given, what supplements and/or medication has been given and where relevant the dosage and whether or not the dragon has gone to the bathroom that day.

At the end of each month you can then write a short summary detailing any possible concerns you may have and any planned actions (i.e. you've noticed ongoing decreased appetite and have booked in a vet consultation to look into this change in behaviour).

At this end of month stage it can also be a good idea to weigh and measure your dragon and note down the weight and length as this can help keep track of how your dragon's growth is going and whether there's any issues with weight such as weight loss or gain.

When taking your dragon to a vet it's great to bring your records book along as your vet can then reference it for a good source of information about how things have been going and what has been done.

Below is an example records excerpt:

DATE	FOOD	SUPPLEMENTS & MEDICINE	PASSED WASTE
30/04/24	Raw green bean 15 mealworms	Calcium + D3 0.1ml Meloxicam orally Chloramphenicol 1% right eye	Y

END OF APRIL

WEIGHT: 512g
LENGTH: 52cm

Continuing to monitor slight swelling in right eye and administering medications as per vets instructions. Since beginning treatment slight improvement has been noted. Appetite is stable and passing of waste is regular with normal appearance. No further concerns.

VETS

I highly recommend Sugarloaf Animal Hospital for any vet care needs in the Newcastle – Hunter Valley region. If you are in need of specialist care for a complex health condition or are located in the Sydney area SASH located in North Ryde also does great work with

reptiles. A healthy dragon will have bright eyes, be alert, the eyes won't appear 'droopy' and the base of the head and tail won't appear sunken in.

Bearded dragons are very good at hiding when they are unwell so often by the time you can **SEE** something is wrong the problem has been going on for a while. This is why it's important to regularly check over your dragon and make note of anything unusual regarding their appearance, appetite and behaviour.

Poop is an important thing to monitor to gain a good idea of the health of your dragon. A healthy dragon will do a solid log that should be green or brown in colour with a white pellet. It should not be soupy or smell extremely bad, this can indicate there's an internal parasite issue. If the white pellet is yellow it is an indicator usually of dehydration or a calcium issue. Provide more water and if the yellowness still persists adjust your calcium supplement routine.

Keep a journal and note down the Date, Food you provided on that day, supplements and medicine (with dosage) provided on that day and whether or not your dragon pooped that day. At the end of each month weigh your dragon and note it down alongside any observations that seem unusual. This is a great way to monitor your dragon's health and if anything does happen is a great resource for the vet to see what's been going on.

Ideally you should schedule a general checkup with a reptile vet once a year right before the start of winter. This helps you to ensure your dragon is healthy enough for brumation and that there's no other issues.

WHAT ABOUT DENTAL CARE?

There has been a recent new recommendation for dental care of reptiles which is to brush their teeth with a reptile safe oral cleaner (Hexarinse or Mavlab). Use a baby toothbrush to brush the teeth. This may be difficult to do but is **VERY** important. Bearded dragons have a unique tooth structure. The teeth along the sides of their mouth are fused **DIRECTLY** to their jawbone which makes them more susceptible to dental issues if proper oral care isn't provided. The teeth should be a cream/bone colour and if you see dark coloration a vet should check it out as it may need a thorough clean or be an indication of a dental issue (i.e. Mouth Rot, Osteomyelitis of the jaw).

Additionally diet plays a role in maintaining your Dragon's dental health. A diet that will assist in good dental health contains foods such as fibrous greens like raw green beans and the avoidance of foods that are higher in acidity and sugars such as fruits. You can limit fruits and berries to just an occasional special treat however if your dragon already has poor dental health it is recommended to cut out fruits and berries completely.

OTHER INFORMATION

- Bearded Dragons are a highly interactive and very intelligent reptile, they have been proven to be able to learn from observing both their own species and other species and will benefit from regular handling and interaction. They often enjoy watching TV and having some supervised roaming time in a secure room of the house or looking out a window.

- Bearded dragons have excellent colour vision which aids them in identifying and selecting food.

- Additionally bearded dragons have a literal third eye located on top of their head between and slightly behind their two main eyes. This eye is small and very basic and has a retina. It is known as a 'Parietal eye' and while it does not see like a regular eye it is capable of picking up on changes in light and shadow (hence why you shouldn't use heat bulbs that emit any coloured light) and is thought to act as a defence that allows the dragon to perceive potential threats from above like a bird of prey.

- A good source of further information is Bearded Dragon forums online. I highly recommend checking out **beardeddragon.org** this is an active forum with members who are owners, veterinarians or enthusiasts where you can ask a variety of questions on different topics and receive answers, support and advice from the community. This forum also has great charts listing which fruits and vegetables are safe to give your dragon alongside how frequently they can be given and how to prepare them.

ABOUT THE AUTHOR

I have always had a passion for animals, particularly those less likely to be everyone's first choice to share their home with as pets.

I have two dragons of my own, both rescues who I have worked with to rehabilitate back to good condition and who feature in some of the photographs in this guide. I also hold certificates in Herpetology and Reptile zoology.

In recent years dragons have become a more popular choice for pets though information about their care is scarce to come by.

I wrote this guide to compile a range of information in a single source to address this issue.

I would like to thank the wonderful staff of Sugarloaf Animal Hospital who agreed to review my drafts to ensure all information contained is accurate, up to date and veterinarian approved.

I hope that you, the reader, find this guide useful and it helps you to enjoy many years with a healthy, happy dragon companion.

– Jordan Bonner, Spike & Puff